I Like Shapes!

by Chris MacCaulay

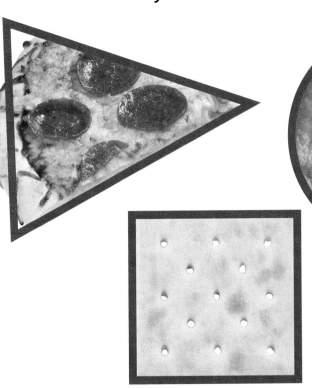

(tl)Don Farrall/Getty Images; (b)Jacques Cornell photographer/McGraw-Hill Education; (tr)©D. Hurst/Alamy

I like  tomatoes.

I like  buns.

3

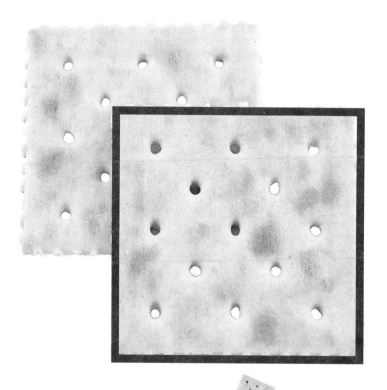

I like crackers.

I like bread.

I like  sandwiches.

I like pizza.

I like cheese.

8